HONEST DIALOGUE

of related interest

Tools for Helpful Souls
Especially for highly sensitive people who provide help
either on a professional or private level
Ilse Sand
ISBN 978 1 78592 296 1
eISBN 978 1 78450 599 8

The Emotional Compass
How to Think Better about Your Feelings
Ilse Sand
ISBN 978 1 78592 127 8
eISBN 978 1 78450 392 5

Getting Better at Getting People Better
Creating Successful Therapeutic Relationships
Noah Karrasch
ISBN 978 1 84819 239 3
eISBN 978 0 85701 186 2

HONEST DIALOGUE

*Presence, Common Sense and Boundaries
when You Want to Help Someone*

Bent Falk

Jessica Kingsley *Publishers*
London and Philadelphia

First published in 2018
by Jessica Kingsley Publishers
73 Collier Street
London N1 9BE, UK
and
400 Market Street, Suite 400
Philadelphia, PA 19106, USA

www.jkp.com

Library of Congress Cataloging in Publication Data
A CIP catalog record for this book is available from the Library of Congress

British Library Cataloguing in Publication Data
A CIP catalogue record for this book is available from the British Library

ISBN 978 1 78592 353 1
eISBN 978 1 78450 689 6

Printed and bound by CPI Group (UK) Ltd, Croydon, CR0 4YY

For
Todd Burley,
mentor and friend

CONTENTS

PREFACE

This book was originally commissioned by the Danish Nursing Association and first published in 1996 in Danish. Its background, still apparent in some places, was my work as a hospital chaplain and teacher of student nurses where I was working at the time, the St. Luke Hospital in Copenhagen, and at other hospitals and nursing schools in Denmark and the other Nordic countries. In subsequent editions, the book's scope was expanded because it had also become popular among professional helpers outside the hospital world, such as teachers, clergy and attorneys.

Readers of the book say their interest is in its grounding in practice, with role play and examples that are easily recognizable from their own working experiences. At the same time, it has a clearly stated theoretical foundation. It is

Gestalt therapeutic, that is, phenomenological, existential, and dialogical. Phenomenological means: with an emphasis on perception and a distinction between perception and interpretation. Existential means: with an emphasis on awareness leading to responsible choices. Dialogical means: exploring rather than lecturing and inviting rather than invading. I have made a determined effort to explain these concepts in a way that makes their practical implications clear, while being aware that I have not been able to exhaust the subject in the limited space available.

The present English edition is based on my own translation—or, rather, rewriting—of the Danish text. It was proofread and polished by my classmate from Wittenberg University (Ohio) and life-long friend, Janice Miriam Schiestl, M.A., Senior Lecturer, Department of English Studies, Innsbruck University. I cannot thank her enough for her dedicated and tireless effort to clarify what I meant to say and, when necessary, keep me on the straight and narrow path of writing style consistency.

I also want to thank the following:

- My agent and former trainee, Ilse Sand, herself an internationally published writer, who helped establish my contact with Jessica Kingsley Publishers. Her energy and trust in my project has been instrumental in bringing it about.

- My teacher, trainer, and friend, the late Todd Burley, Ph.D. from Gestalt Associates Training, Los Angeles (GATLA), who read an early draft of my English text and encouraged me to go on with it.

• And last, but not least, my patient and always supportive therapist colleague and wife, Inger, who during the months of my intensive work with the English edition, on top of tending to her own practice, was doing my share of what we need to do to keep our household going—feeding me great meals, cleaning, shopping, entertaining, paying the bills, supporting me, and sharing with me a tear of joy or two whenever there was progress.

Hellerup, Denmark
March 21, 2017

I

Introduction

p.13

1 TECHNIQUE OR ATTITUDE

The purpose of this book is to offer a practical approach to what might be called "the technique of dialogue" but would be better termed "the *art* of dialogue." The art—facilitated by certain techniques—is to create *contact*, and contact is established through *awareness* and *authentic presence*. This art, like any other skill, must be learned through practice and is learnt most effectively under knowledgeable supervision of that practice. A book on the subject of dialogue helps to prepare for the practical process and for the possible supervision of that process by someone who has the vantage point of not being directly involved in it.

This book advocates an attitude of flexible responsibility, that is, *response-ability*, guided by a, in the positive sense of the word, naïve awareness. It does not offer absolutely "right" solutions or answers. There is not likely to be one unambiguously right answer to an individual person's problems, and if there were, such an answer could not be given by someone else independent of the *experience* of the one asking for guidance. Genuine dialogue is an occurrence (process) of contact between two or more people. It requires surrender to the reality of what *is* according to the respective perceptions of the people in the encounter at that particular moment in time. That is why no response is always right, and none always wrong. "Always wrong" though, is an attitude of always wanting to "get it right" rather than going with what is spontaneous and real.

The book is intended as an inspiration to awareness about the practice of encounter. Thus, it draws its material from practice. It is based on my Copenhagen-based work as a psychotherapist, teacher, trainer, and supervisor of individual clients and groups, in particular with church and hospital staff. In other words, even though no statement or example in the book is meant to represent the ultimate *solution* to any patient's or client's "problem," no such statement or example is so unusual or provocative that it has not proven itself useful. It is, therefore, my hope that the book, in its brevity, may raise the awareness, and broaden the range, of possible interventions for the open-minded reader.

2 CRISIS

Crisis is a reaction to a loss or the threat of a loss of something that has meaning—that is, value—for the person concerned. It may be the loss of something tangible and concrete— an object—or something mental or spiritual, such as self-esteem or trust in God. Often it is a combination of both in that the loss of ability or a loved one turns out to have a strong symbolic meaning for the person in crisis. The loss of physical health, for example, may be experienced as a loss of love, freedom, and self-worth.

The word "crisis" stems from the Greek word *krinein*, which means "to judge." This indicates that crisis is linked with (re)evaluation, values, and choice. So, crisis is not just a misfortune. Times of crisis may also be times of growth. In the face of change—positive or negative—our previous life patterns and understanding may turn out to be more or less inadequate. Extremely disturbing and anxiety-provoking as that may be, it may also be an impetus for growth and progress.

Crisis may be caused by a reduction of life's possibilities, as, for example, when someone loses a body part or a close relative. But it may also be caused by the fact that we have expanded and have come to be greater or stronger, as in puberty or when we move away from our parents' home. In both cases, we acquire eyes that see and ears that hear things to which habit had blinded us before. In both cases, the crisis calls for new visions and new creativity in us. Thus, crisis is not just an illness that needs to be cured; it is life that needs to be lived. To a person in crisis, help is therefore not a matter of treatment or the giving of advice. Crisis intervention is helping someone to *grow* according to his/her own capacities and values, and this is done by helping that person access those capacities and values through an increased awareness of them.

In considering how one human being may help to bring about that kind of growth in another, it is important to acknowledge that the helper can only do this in an *indirect* way. What is involved here is "the paradoxical theory of change," as formulated by the psychiatrist and preeminent Gestalt therapist Arnold Beisser (see Chapter 10). It states that people do not really change as long as they try to be what they are *not* but only when they fully identify with what they *are*.

This implies that what you *are* is primary to and therefore more important than what you *do*. In order to facilitate full contact, it is important that the helper:

- is present and available as the helper he/she *is*; in practice that means that he/she is open about what he/she wants and does not want at any point in the dialogue

- respectfully attends to who the helpee is; in practice, that means being open to what the helpee wants and does not want at any point in the dialogue

- respectfully shares with the helpee relevant pieces of information about what happens to him/herself (the helper) during the encounter.

"Full contact" in the therapeutic sense is a contact between two people that is sufficiently based on their respective realities to have a healing potential. It happens when both parties are consistently clear about what they want to give and get at the contact interface. Fortunately, if just one of the two lead the way into such clarity, it will often encourage the other person (helper, helpee or any other important person in one's life) to do the same. It takes two to manipulate but only one to stop it. If, for example, both insist that they are right and try to convince the other of that, they are having a war. If just one of them can live with being wrong occasionally, or at least with the difference of opinion between them, they have peace. Or, if both want to be "good enough" in some absolute sense, they have a war. If just one of them remains grounded in the observable fact that he/she is good enough to be alive in the world such as he/she and the world are, even though he/she is not good enough to provide what that person wants from him/her at that particular point, they will both have peace. Also, the dissatisfied one will probably have learned something important from the one who is basically satisfied with being better than nothing.

3 ANXIETY AND PRIMARY FEELINGS

Anxiety as a result of repression
The experience of being in crisis is first and foremost one of anxiety. Part of that anxiety is caused by repression and will ease as the afflicted person discovers and identifies with his/her primary feelings (emotions) and wants (or "needs" as standard psycho-speak would have it) and makes relevant decisions concerning them. The primary feelings are glad, sad, angry ("mad"), and afraid. They are primary in the sense that one or more of them is involved in all the states of mind that we generally call "feelings," often without distinguishing clearly between emotions, sensations, thoughts, preferences, opinions, intuitions, and attitudes. The primary feelings may be compared to the primary colors, which, in different concentrations and mixtures, make up all the other colors. The other components of our more complex "feelings" are cognitive materials, such as

the memories, thoughts, hopes, and fears that arise when we *think* about the particular experience. The "feeling" of patriotism (love for one's country), for example, is a complex phenomenon that like any other kind of love may contain any one, or any combination, of the four primary emotions. We are glad when we return to our country; we are sad when we have to leave it, and we are angry or afraid when others threaten it (see Chapter 12).

It is important to see, hear, acknowledge ("support"), and ask about primary feelings, both in ourselves as helpers and in those who are seeking help. Primary feelings indicate direction and intensity for the psychic energy and lead to the decisive question: "What do you *want?*" When you are aware and take responsibility for what you *feel* (not just what you *ought* to feel) and *want* (not just what you *should* want), and when you express it to your partner in a dialogue, then you are alive and present with that person. In this way, you automatically help your partner to gain a similar kind of awareness/responsibility for him/herself, which is a help in growing through the crisis.

Existential anxiety

Repression of primary feelings and of wants causes anxiety. This aspect of the anxiety eases when a person becomes aware of what he/she truly feels and wants and makes up his/her mind about what to do with it. Even the awareness of the primary emotion of fear is a relief compared with anxiety, because fear is concrete and relates to a specific situation, whereas anxiety tends to be unfocused, generalized, and exaggerated. However, there is also a part of the anxiety that does not disappear through consciousness-raising. This may be called *existential* because it is an unchangeable condition for our existence as human beings. Our time of life

ANXIETY AND PRIMARY FEELINGS

is limited and uncertain. Our contacts with others are at best partial, and we never know when we will lose them again. We have to make choices and carry the responsibility/guilt for them. And we have to do it more or less blindfolded, for we do not know the future circumstances that we are attempting to prepare for. How will the weather be tomorrow? What will our lover be like in 20 years?

My uncertainty about what I feel and want at a given moment might be diminished by dialogue in aware ("full") contact (as opposed to an absent-minded, mindless party conversation, for example) with another person. This would do away with, or at least reduce, the part of the anxiety that arises from the very attempt to control it. However, an amount of uncertainty about the future will remain as an inescapable condition for our existence, even though this *existential anxiety* at times may recede into the background. In other words, existential anxiety is not a disease and there is no treatment for it. It is, on the contrary, a kind of sanity: it comes from having discovered just how uncontrollable life really is. All we can do not to drown in this awareness is to face it and commit ourselves to the life we have while we still have it. This gives a direction for helping the anxious person. The principle is helping him/her *into* his/her reality rather than *out* of it. When we try to repress existential anxiety, we only come to compound the basic problem with an effort that in itself gives rise to anxiety, and thus we end up with two problems instead of one. Anxiety comes from "not being where you are," as the American psychiatrist and psychotherapist Fritz Perls put it.

The following chapter will explore more deeply what has already been said about a contact-enabling approach to people seeking help in crises of life and in more everyday situations of communication difficulties.

II

Practical Guidelines

---

p.23

4   IT IS LESS COMPLICATED THAN YOU THINK

Even though a specific subject may be complicated, the dialogue concerning it does not need to be so. If it feels hard to communicate, it is not because the subject matter is difficult in itself but because there are aspects of it that you are trying to avoid.

Simple or easy

"Simple" does not necessarily mean "easy." If it seems difficult for someone to help in a particular situation, then it is as difficult for him/her as it is experienced, and that should not be dismissed. However, it is important to be precise in stating what the difficulty is. When it is hard to carry on an existential dialogue, it is not because it is complicated. There is nothing complicated about agreeing with a patient that it is sad that he/she must die at an early age. Or, if there is,

24

something may be done to make it less complicated. The task of agreeing with the obvious is in itself very simple, and it only comes to be "complicated" at the point where, for some reason, the helper wants to avoid part of what is obvious. It is, indeed, difficult to talk in a way that would diminish the sadness of an early death. A relevant program of training and supervision might help a helper to realize this and thus do away with the "complicated" part of carrying on a helping dialogue with someone in a painful state of circumstances and mind. A very different kind of difficulty, however, is the emotional burden of being with the other person in his/her distress and with the burden of your own inability to make the other person's suffering disappear.

These burdens are inherent and unavoidable in the helping contact. They call for a kind of training and supervision that helps the helper not to be confluent (flowing together) with the person in need. It is important to be aware of who it is that suffers from what at this very moment and who it is that is responsible for doing what about it. However, it is not the purpose and, it is hoped, also not in the power of any training of helping professionals to turn the helping person into someone who doesn't care at all. You do care, or you would have chosen another profession. In moderation, it might even be helpful that you share with the other person something about what you see and hear and something about your reaction to that. For instance, it would be simple (though not necessarily easy) to say, "I really wish I could help you with this, *and* right now I do not see how!"

If a helper thinks that it is "difficult" to inquire into what the helpee experiences, wants, and wants to do about it, it is often because there is some part of it that the helper him/herself fears or disagrees with (moralizes about). There is nothing complicated about that either, but it does become complicated when you try to disguise your discomfort, dislike, or disagreement from the one you are helping. Contact is based on the awareness of difference. It makes no one less lonely to talk to his/her own image in the mirror.

Helping is not always giving advice
If you think that the difficulty in addressing an issue comes from its complicated nature, it may be because you are confusing the existential/spiritual dialogue with giving advice. If you want to find advice for the other person, talking with him/her tends to be quite complicated. You do not know the other person's values and you are not necessarily more clever than him/her. You also do not wield more power than him/her over life, death, love, loss, or guilt. Finally, you will often experience a frustrating resistance in the other person to following your advice, even when the other person has explicitly asked for it! This pattern is called "appeal and rejection," and it has turned hairs gray on many a helper's head. However, if you experience this kind of behavior in someone seeking help, you need not despair of your inabilities or powerlessness. And you need not be angry with the other person for putting you in that ego-shattering situation; rather, you may smile at your own obsession with trying to be clever (in the eye of the other) and with gaining power (over the other's life). That is actually a form of megalomania. Perhaps you could tell the other person something about this insight, thus demonstrating a redeeming capacity for taking yourself seriously *and* not solemnly. Something like this, perhaps:

"I am aware that I have fallen into the temptation of offering advice, and I know that you can no more make use of other people's experiences than I can, so I am going to stop it."

This is in principle simple, although in practice it may be (emotionally) difficult for certain helpers at certain times, such as: when asking the helpee about *primary emotions* (joy, sorrow, anger, and fear); when asking the helpee, "What do you *want* (wish and hope for)?"; when asking the helpee, "What are you *doing* about it?"; when telling the helpee, in relevant amounts, what *you* feel and want as far as the present contact is concerned, and what you are actually doing in order to help him/her.

Personal and private

It should be noted that the useful information about the helper's experience is that which applies directly to the *present situation*. Details of the helper's own history outside of the present contact are, in contrast, usually disruptive. When this distinction is maintained, the dialogue may become *personal* without becoming *private*. The person who is being helped is unlikely to be interested for very long in the helper's personal life or past. It also does not work for the helper to try to establish some sense of "solidarity" with the helpee by recounting his/her own problems and how he/she dealt with them. It may well be perceived as condescending by the sufferer and almost certainly as an interruption. So, beyond an occasional, brief, illustrative example for the sake of clarifying a point of communication, the helper should not steal the story and the time from the one seeking (and paying for) help.

5   THE ESSENTIAL RESOURCES

The essential resources for overcoming a difficulty are in the person having the difficulty or in the field of interaction between the people in dialogue. The helper is the interpreter and facilitator of the helpee's search for clarification and choice. You are not the one to make the choices or "fix" things for the other person.

What is essential?

Some of the resources to overcome a difficulty are within the helper, but the essential, *decisive* resources are within the person having the difficulty. The primary objective for the helping encounter is that the help seeker comes to be aware of the issues of his/her life and takes responsibility for them. In other words, what is decisive is that the person makes his/her own decisions about what to do or stop doing. At best, the helper may contribute to this process of awareness and choice with his/her empathy, focused questioning, and life experience. These contributions are, indeed, important resources for the helpee, but only his/her decision is decisive.

Other important features of the supporting process are often overlooked because they are in neither the helper nor the help seeker. They are in, or rather *of*, the field consisting of both of them and the interaction between them, an interaction in which both persons are at the same time and all of the time both cause and effect of what goes on. This field functions as a whole, all aspects of which touch upon (affect) one another, in which changing one part changes the entire field. In this field-theoretical perspective, both (all) the participants in the encounter are seen as active, in contrast to an understanding of the helping contact where one person—the helper—is seen as doing something *to* another—the person seeking help. The space between the partners in dialogue is active and not passive or empty. That is to say, the encounter creates new knowledge and new ideas that neither of the participants would have arrived at alone. It is in this way that you experience the valuable dialogue: it is the relationship, as the third entity between the partners, that enriches both (all) of them.

6   GOOD HELP IS HELP
       TOWARDS SELF-HELP

All other help is intrusion. When you take responsibility for someone, you take responsibility from that person. It is better to teach the hungry to fish than to feed him or her a fish.

Help: an ambiguous commodity

It is a common view that help is always a good thing, which would mean the helpee would get as much of it as possible and the helper would give as much of it as possible. In that way, the helper easily gets stuck in a squeeze between perpetual bad conscience on one side and exhaustion on the other, and the helpee gets stuck in the role of the appealing or injured victim. This is not good for any of the persons involved. In other words, help is not only a good thing, just as medication is not only a good thing. Both have side effects, and too much of either is poisonous. When you take responsibility *for* another person, you by the same token take responsibility *from* him/her, and that may provide some symptomatic relief, but in the long run it does not really help. If you support someone else in the habit of allowing others to take responsibility for things that he/she might be able to do, you undermine his/her initiative and life proficiency. You thereby end up increasing the other person's existential anxiety, which in turn heightens his/her appeal for help, and thus a vicious circle is established.

It may turn out better if you help as little as possible *and* as much as necessary, which means only as much as it takes for the person in need to regain balance and orientation in his/her own life. This way the help will be a help to help oneself, i.e. an impetus to grow, rather than an invitation to regress, meaning the return to a less mature level of functioning. In an acute situation, "as little as possible" may in fact be quite a lot, but that does not take away from the principle that the helpee should, as soon as possible, take over as much responsibility as possible for his/her own life.

Helper syndrome or "burn-out"
It is important that the helper is aware of his/her own wants ("needs") for succor and help, otherwise so-called "helper syndrome" might develop. That means that the helper *transfers* (projects) his/her longings and desires onto the helpee and tries to help him/herself by proxy through the other.

Neither person is helped by this. For the helper, it may lead to a one-sided and rigid encounter in which he/she insists on helping the other in precisely his/her own way and at his/her own pace and construes it as a personal failure (narcissistic injury) if he/she fails. This may in turn lead to a state of burn-out in the helper, which is characterized, among other things, by a sense of rejection, depression, and low self-esteem. Additionally, in the person being helped, it may cause a considerable amount of (hidden) resentment and therefore resistance to the situation. The overbearing attitude of the helper is perceived by the person in need as a denial of his/her autonomy: he/she is not seen, heard, or respected, with his/her own real issues and personality.

It may be difficult for the helper to change a habit of trying to help too much because the pattern is supported by idealized notions of kindness and love of humanity. The helper may get praise and prestige by doing as much good for the other person as possible, rather than doing as little as possible in order for the other person to be able to help him/herself. In reality, however, helping in order for the helper to look good is turning the other person into a means rather than an end. When the sufferer is being used by the rescuer to maintain for him/herself a certain (stereotype) self-image as The Good Helper, it is selfishness in disguise.

The best way for the helper to avoid this pattern is through self-awareness and a non-judgmental (non-moralistic) approach to his/her own wants. You might, for instance, choose to understand your fatigue merely as a need for rest (description), rather than as "laziness" or "weakness" (evaluation). The paradox is that you help the other person best when you take your own wants seriously. That means that you take direct action to get what you do want or do not want, instead of repressing your wishes or trying to get them fulfilled indirectly through manipulation. As a minimum, you state your wishes (preferences) in clear language rather than playing a guessing game, so you do not turn the other person into your substitute, doing what you as the helper so far have been unable to do for yourself, such as "grieve" or "grow up." In provocative terms, the best helper might be said to be exactly what most helpers fear being called, i.e. ignorant, lazy, and selfish. *Ignorant* in that you seek information about the problem from the only one who knows—the helpee—instead of thinking you already know or know better. Lazy in that you do not do for the other what he/she might be able to do and would benefit from doing for him/herself. And selfish in the sense of being authentically present as the person you are, rather than the one you "ought" to be.

The truly good helper may well be an intelligent and hardworking person devoted to the service of people in need, but, paradoxically, to do good often takes doing something bad. The unlimited good comes to be evil (destructive) in that it is unreal and unbelievable, and it encourages an addiction to other-support rather than self-support in the help seeker. So, the good helper does as little as possible *for* the other person, and he/she is true to him/herself in the contact. That means being transparent with his/her own wants and his/her own limitations, both of which he/she shares with the helpee in relevant amounts (clinical judgment) and without being overly self-critical (moralistic) about it. If, as a helper, you do not dare to be human, you are not trustworthy and you have no real warmth for the other person.

7   WHEN, AS THE HELPER, YOU DON'T KNOW WHAT TO SAY OR DO, THAT IS WHAT YOU SHOULD SAY OR DO

To be speechless and confused is also part of reality, and reality is always our best friend.

The "negative" is the most trustworthy

Many professional helpers who use dialogue as a tool wish always to be able to "say something" to the one in need. At the same time, many think that this is "difficult," in the sense of "complicated." In *reality*, it is always simple to be able to say something; it only requires that you do not exclude the "negative" statements from all possible answers. That would be answers like "I don't know…," "I can't…," "I will not…," I don't think…," "I do not believe…," and answers that contain the so-called "negative" feelings, "I am angry, sad, or afraid." If you think that you *must* say something even when you have nothing to say that would make the difference you want, there is always the possibility of saying,

"I don't know what to say about that," or, "I can't think of anything to say that would make you feel better." Or you might ask, "What would you want to hear from me right now?" Or you might tell the helpee something about how it impacts you to hear and see what he/she is telling or showing you at this moment.

Again, if you as the helper find this "difficult," it is because there is something about it you are trying to avoid. It is not because it is complicated. Maybe you do not like your own confusion or powerlessness. Or maybe you do not like giving up your self-image as the endlessly kind person. Or maybe you fear encountering the anger of the other when you disappoint his/her expectations or challenge him/her. That, however, may also be addressed in the dialogue! If you admit to the other person that you hate or are sad about the fact that you can't solve his/her problem for him/her, you stop your vanity from blocking you (making you speechless). At the same time, you have demonstrated a confidence-building honesty in the contact. Our "weaknesses" are the most trustworthy parts of us because no one would suspect the helper of lying to make him/herself appear worse than he/she is, whereas it is easy to imagine that someone would lie about him/herself to make him/herself look better than he/she is.

A final advantage of the helper's admission of his/her limitations is that it makes it easier for the helpee to admit to his/her own limitations and live with them. It is hard to forgive yourself when faced with a perfect or almighty person. Thus, again and again, it turns out that what *redeems* the dialogue and the people in it from whatever stops it at the threshold of healing contact are the character traits and skills that, so to speak, lie in the shadow of the stereotypical image of the good helper and form a counter-image to it.

Attempts to hide the shadow will, conversely, make for a shallow, two-dimensional contact—like a picture without any shadow effects. It is not possible to censor away some part of yourself—the "negative"—without the encounter being censored all together, which will take the life out of it.

Whose pain is it?
It is simple (but not necessarily easy) to find out what to say when you do not know what to say. It is equally simple to find out what to do when you do not know what to do. Then you do nothing—aside from maybe stating that this is what you can say or do and why. Many helpers fear being powerless and have perhaps chosen a helping profession precisely in an attempt to overcome their own painful experiences with powerlessness. It may indeed be awful not to be able to do anything about another's pain, but this should not paralyze the helper or make him/her speechless. It is what is awful for the helpee that should be in focus.

8   DON'T LET HAVING A PROBLEM TURN INTO A PROBLEM

If you do, you will have two problems instead of one

If you do not allow yourself to experience and talk about the negative parts of reality, the dialogue will be confusing and full of holes where there is no contact (see Chapter 2). That does not change whatever is negative; the help seeker is just left alone with it. If you are powerless, you have a problem as far as getting what you want. And if you don't admit it, you have two!

If you turn the state of being powerless into a problem in itself, you have doubled the problem (see Chapter 7). This also applies to a number of other events or situations when you try to change that which cannot be changed (the *existential* pain) and double the problem by your fight against the inevitable. There are hardships that the helping dialogue cannot remove—illness, pain, guilt, anxiety, loneliness, and powerlessness—but the helper may help the helpee not to compound his/her suffering with self-reproach ("I am a failure because I have no power"). When you turn having a problem into a problem, you double the problem. When you accept the problem, you cut it in half. This is what Sigmund Freud called, "turning neurotic suffering into ordinary suffering."

Lack of power may be very unpleasant, but there is also an advantage to it that is often overlooked. That which you cannot do is obviously also that which you must not do. "Should" and "ought" are silenced in the face of an absolute impossibility. To be powerless is also to be free of guilt in the particular situation. This might be worth considering when you are in the above-mentioned trap between exhaustion and bad conscience.

9 BOUNDARIES CONSTITUTE CONTACT

Take another person's hand, and you will know what this means. Where you end and the other begins, i.e. in the palms of your respective hands, is where the two of you touch.

The boundaries mutually define you and the other person. Boundaries have multiple functions: they divide, they join, and they define, and these are three aspects of the same thing. The word "define" is derived from the Latin *fines*, meaning limits or boundaries. To define something means to differentiate it from other objects or ideas to which it bears some resemblance or to which it is close in time or space. The "negative" aspect of the boundary (the "no" part) is that it spells out what is *not*. This is balanced by the "positive" aspect (the "yes" part) of identifying that which *is*. A clear definition requires both. *Being* and *not being* are mutually dependent. And as the boundary defines two objects or areas by differentiating between them—in a sense, separating them—it also constitutes the interface of contact between them. Contact is where two separate entities touch, such as when you hold another person's hand. The skin of the hands makes up the physical boundary of the respective bodies, and at the same time the skin is where the contact is.

At the level of non-living things, the contact boundary is of vital importance as the point where chemical and electrical reactions occur. And in living organisms, the skin is not just a place where contact may happen, it is an organ of contact, as you realize when you experience the intense emotional impact of a handshake or sometimes merely the touch of a finger.

So, boundaries—limits—are important. The helper's limitations, painful as they may be, are also resources. Boundaries allow the helper and the helpee to be who they really are, which is inextricably linked with who they are *not*. By making our boundaries clear, we make it possible to establish contact even when we cannot provide the kind of help that the helpee had hoped for. The helper cannot help the helpee acquire a new childhood or partner, but when the helper admits to his/her helplessness it makes room for statements like these:

> "It makes me angry to hear how badly they have treated you."

> "It doesn't sound as if there is much dignity left for either of you in the way you talk to each other."

The helper cannot change death as a part of life for all of us. But when he/she faces it, there is room to share grief over the human condition with the other:

"Yes, it is terrible that we have to die."

In the above examples, there is no longer anything that anyone can do; the boundary has been reached. But despite this, the people in the dialogue may still meet as human beings who reveal important and relevant parts of their experience in the contact. They share the boundaries of human existence as far as life, love, and death are concerned and they share the contact interface of what is happening between them. Boundaries make for contact, and, fortunately, lack of power does not prevent it. It is the other way around: contact is prevented by wanting power in the situation so badly that you get angry or ashamed over your powerlessness and try to hide it from the other person.

Boundary or distance
The necessity of a so-called "professional distance" for the protection of both the helper and the helpee is often emphasized in the training of nurses, pastors, therapists, and counselors. The issues of avoiding confusion of professional and private interests, and confusion of who is helping whom, are indeed important ones. However, the terminology of "distance" may be misleading. It is not so much about being distant, but more about clearly defining the boundaries between the helper and help seeker, not just for protection but also in the interest of contact.

Unclear boundaries require a wide no man's land, such as:

- physical distance, where you want to put a desk between you and the other person or choose to remain standing at the bedside rather than sitting down by the bed or maybe on the bed itself

- emotional distance, where the dialogue is hampered by non-spontaneous expressions, secrets, and hidden agendas

- distance to the other person's problems. If the helper does not acknowledge and express his/her own limitations, for instance his/her inability to turn death into a pleasant event or his/her unwillingness to spend more time with a particular helpee at the particular moment, there will be a range of subjects that are not allowed to come up in the dialogue, which will turn it into two monologues.

In contrast, having clear boundaries makes it possible to get close to each other, as the following examples show:

"I cannot see how I can solve your problem, and I do want to listen to what you have to say."

"I will stay for another 15 minutes, although I am off work for today. When those 15 minutes are up, I will leave. (It is important here not to say that you have to leave because that would be an attempt to obscure that there is a choice involved, which both parties are very well aware of.) We can talk again tomorrow if you want to."

"No thanks, I will not come and visit you at home. First, I cannot do that with all my clients/patients and second, it will always be a different relationship if we move out of the setting we have here. You are welcome to come back and visit me/us here, if you wish."

"It is fine with me to hold your hand for a while, and I will not give you a hug. At this point it would be getting too close for me."

Yes and no are mutually dependent

The above examples of setting limits have the following in common: the helper clearly states both what he/she wants and does not want. Yes and no, will and will not, are mutually dependent. Both are required to establish clear boundaries. The boundary has, by definition, two sides: one that faces the other person (the *yes* side) and one that faces away from the other person (the *no* side, see Chapter 7). When the helpee knows what he/she can and cannot get, he/she is likely to be satisfied with what he/she can get while it is available. Then both parties are freed from the manipulation and boundary testing that occur when the helpee attempts to get more service than what is available and the helper wants to give less but is too "polite" to be clear about it. When yes and no (will/will not) are clearly stated, the boundaries of the people involved are experienced as contact and not rejection.

43

10 YOU CANNOT CHANGE
WHAT YOU DO NOT ACCEPT

This is true with "change" in the sense of psychological and spiritual growth. A person grows only when he/she feels fundamentally accepted as he/she is.

The paradoxical theory of change

The title of this chapter was formulated by the analytical psychologist C. G. Jung and expresses a vital point of psychotherapeutic knowledge (Jung 1948). It is similar to what the psychiatrist and Gestalt therapist Arnold Beisser calls the "paradoxical theory of change," which he describes in this way: "People do not change as long as they try to be what they are *not*, but only when they fully identify with what they *are*" (Beisser 1971, p.1) (see Chapter 2). It is a paradox, i.e. an apparent self-contradiction, that you may become what you are already, and it is a paradox that the person who would want you to change must give up trying to do it in order for the change to—perhaps—happen. However, when we speak of aspects of upbringing, psychological and spiritual growth, and mutual influence in married couples, it becomes easier to comprehend what the theory implies. An upbringing that is carried out in an atmosphere of non-acceptance or under threat of the loss of acceptance/love may lead to some kind of change, but not growth. A healthy upbringing involves setting limits and ensures that actions are seen to have consequences in a naturally consistent way. But the threat of loss of love, i.e. a sense of *conditional* acceptance, will lead only to a superficial adaptation to the demands of the situation. There will be a tendency to "cheat," or to hide your true self, whenever possible, along with hidden or overt rebelliousness. A couple's growth towards a more satisfactory relationship cannot happen under the pressure of the threat of abandonment either. If one partner does not trust the other partner's basic acceptance of him/herself as a person (what you *are*), he/she will not develop a self-sustaining desire (a desire from within) to change his/her behavior (what you *do*) towards satisfying the other person's wants. Without the basic (basically unconditional) acceptance, you might at best change out of fear, with all the negative consequences of that in a close relationship.

This corresponds on the inner level as: if you try to "improve" yourself without having a basic acceptance of yourself as a person, you will discover that the attempt is sabotaged by an inner protest (the "underdog"). Troublesome as this may be when you want to lose weight, stop smoking, or be nice to your mother-in-law, it is in principle a healthy protest against having to "deserve" your existence through achievements. It may also be called a protest against having to *pay for love*. The inner war between "top dog" and "underdog" does not end until you fully identify with both sides and establish a respectful dialogue between them. Only then is a real transformation (growth) towards a more relevant behavior possible, and it should be emphasized that what changes is not what you *are* but what you *do* with what you are.

Change as growth versus change as production

The accepting contact i.e. the contact that is based not on power but on awareness and honesty, is a greenhouse for human growth. Growth is an indirect form of change because you can only help make it possible; thereafter, it either happens by its own power or it doesn't. In addition to being indirect, growth is also a paradoxical change because the organism that changes through growth essentially remains the same. The form will change—as with the corn sprout that springs from the planted seed, or with the adult compared with the child he/she once was—but all the possibilities that unfold during the change were present (more or less hidden) in the organism from the very beginning as what constitutes its *being* as that particular species or person.

It is important to not confuse this organic type of change—growth—with another other type of change that plays a big role in our modern, science-oriented society: *production*. Production effects change directly through the application of power and turning things into what they are not, and the aim of the change is defined, so to speak, from the *outside*, i.e. by the producer, without what is being changed having any say about it.

The effort of making a "productional" change is often but not always relevant to the change that you want. It is relevant in the production of industrial products like cars, washing machines, or other inanimate objects, and it may even be relevant in dealing with human beings. It is perfectly relevant that schools produce readers, and that does require a certain amount of disciplining of the pupils by the teacher (at the "doing" level) at the same time as he/she establishes an accepting atmosphere in the classroom (at the "being" level). And it is relevant that hospitals produce health, which requires many activities other than love and tender care. The process of removing an appendix is not a matter for dialogue with the inflamed organ, but a question of doing to it what it has not asked anyone to do, even if, it is hoped, the patient has. But the production model is not relevant when it comes to dealing with people's existential issues. People who have to make choices about their lives must come to be aware of their own values, not the helper's, and make choices for which they, not the helper, will pay the consequences. That is why all decisive resources for overcoming the difficulty are in the afflicted and not in the helper (see Chapter 5). The helper may at best be a mediator or catalyst for the helpee's own process.

Care and treatment
A special challenge in the helping encounter is that the growth and production models for change may be relevant at the same time. For the nurse, the *treatment* of a patient involves production (doing to) aspects, whereas the *care* for the patient involves growth (being with) aspects. While both go hand in hand in the hospital situation, it is important that they do not get confused. That the patient wishes for his/her appendix to be treated by an expert surgeon does not mean that he also wishes for his/her *existence* to be treated, although he/she might deeply appreciate having someone listen and react to his/her existential issues.

In summary, the helping dialogue should not be contrived or "directed" but should be open. It may be compared to a dance where the music inspires both people's

47

movements, whereas the determination of one person to move in a particular way no matter what would turn the dance into a wrestling match. It is fine to be willing in the sense that you are available for the other person and for the mutual process of communication. To be willing to dialogue facilitates it; the will to control its content or process kills it.

11 THE CONSOLATION IS THAT THERE IS NO CONSOLATION

This means that it consoles no one for very long to lie about their experienced reality. It also means that there is more hope for the humanity in, for example, a mother's inconsolable weeping for her dead child than there would be in a "consolation" that would help her not to care about the loss.

The "awkward" feelings

"Consolation" in the helping dialogue is problematic. In the normal meaning of the word, consolation is an attempt to make awkward, unpleasant feelings such as grief, anger, and fear disappear. Whenever the helper tries to do that, he/she enters into a process of contradicting and disagreeing with ("second guessing") the experience of the help seeker. That means that by idealizing, persuading, making light, and deflecting, he/she tries to get the other person to feel something other than what he/she does feel. The helper may think that those other feelings would be better for the troubled person, but then he/she must at least negotiate that with the helpee rather than try to dictate or manipulate the other person to change his/her experience as in, "Be brave!" or, "You have to set a good example!" In truth, it is usually for the sake of the helper that he/she is trying to make the other person "feel better." Better for whom?

Feelings are medicine, not illness
If the helper really were to succeed in changing the help seeker's experience through contradiction, it would merely be symptomatic relief. It would be confusing the cause (for example a loss) with the effect (grief) in order for the helper to avoid meeting the grief, anger, or fear of the other person. What we feel comes from what we *perceive*, and that which we perceive comes from the reality we are part of. Our *interpretation* of what we perceive might be modified by our habitual (perhaps pathological) thinking and imagination to a degree where it is not valid (optimal) in the particular situation. In such a case, the helping dialogue may help to change the emotions *indirectly* (not by dictation or second guessing) by working with the interpretation of what the patient is hearing and seeing. For example, you might inform a patient that cancer does not always mean immediate death or that the death process does not always involve physical pain. But often, as a helper, you cannot change the painful reality itself by offering some kind of cure or treatment. And you cannot change any part of reality by not calling it by its right name.

The other person is (it is hoped) *right* in that his/her pain is meaningless or "not fair." If you try to remove (forbid) such *relevant* feelings/evaluations in the suffering person, you do him/her a disservice. It is appropriate to grieve after a loss, to be angry when you are abused, to fear when you are confronted with the unknown or when your wellbeing is threatened, so it is not the feelings in themselves that are problematic if they are proportional to the reality. It is the *reality* that may be a "problem" (burden). Facing reality, however hard it is, helps you to cope with it, and not suppressing your emotions saves psychic energy. Feelings are not disease, they are medicine. Joy helps us to receive, sorrow helps us to let go, anger helps us to set limits (getting what we want and not getting what we do not want), and fear helps us to escape a danger that might damage or kill us. So, all the primary emotions are *life* and help with being alive (orienting yourself in life according to your wants).

It is the contact that consoles
What consoles the most is when the afflicted person is allowed to feel what he/she feels without having it "consoled" away. Rejection of another person's feelings creates distance. "Don't be so upset" functions as "You are wrong to be feeling what you feel," and "I don't want to be with you in your grief." That also goes for the so-called "feeling" (*experience*) that the habitual comforter usually has the most difficulty with— the experience in the helpee of not being "good enough." If the helper responds with a denial such as "Oh yes you are," it makes the other person experience that he/she is not only inferior but also lonesome (abandoned) (see Chapter 10). If, on the other hand, the helper allows for the experience of the helpee, he/she will enable a *contact* between the two of them that does comfort the helpee. When two people together look at one of life's difficulties and acknowledge it as a challenge or a burden, the difficulty becomes easier to cope with and live with. This is often all that one person can do to help another, and it is no minor achievement.

And there is another, just as important, aspect to the statement that "The consolation is that there is no consolation." If it were possible to comfort a mother who just lost her child in a traffic accident so that she no longer grieved, it would be a desolation worse than grief. It would mean that people are not important and love is not important. Grief is homeless love, and it would be a double loss for the grieving person to have his/her love "consoled" away.

12 THE PERSON IN DISTRESS DOES NOT NEED CONSOLATION, BUT LOVE

Love is, functionally, not a feeling, but a relationship that confirms that I exist and am welcome in the world. Interestingly, even an angry confrontation may serve as that kind of confirmation. Confirming someone's existence is done through the process: I see you, I hear you, I respond (tell you what I see and hear and tell you something about how it impacts me). Conclusion: to love is to see, hear, and respond.

Love is not a feeling but a relationship that causes feelings

In the previous section, a distinction was made between true and false consolation, and true consolation was defined as a *contact* that draws upon mutual acknowledgement of the given reality. Another way of putting it is that true comfort is *love*. Then, however, it becomes necessary to be precise in the definition of what love means in the context of a helping contact, in contrast to its sentimental/romantic meaning in certain other connections.

Love, as mentioned in Chapter 3, is not one or more *feelings*; it is a relationship in which you unconditionally validate the other person and seek to further his/her life and growth. "Unconditionally" means that your support of the other person is not contingent upon speculation (rules) about what he/she *deserves* but based on observation of what he/she needs in order to be able to "support" him/herself. "Support" as a Gestalt therapeutic technical term means what a person needs in order to identify with what he/she wants and fears (his/her motivation and resistance) and to take responsible action concerning these foci of energy. You may give that kind of support of the life of another person to someone without very much *emotional* involvement in him/her and even to someone whom you do not particularly like. "Love your enemy" should not be misunderstood as a demand to make yourself feel certain feelings. That would be absurd because our feelings, as well as our wants and any other part of our *being*, are not subject to the control of our willpower. Instead, the idea or commandment is about *doing*. It is about doing to the other person what you would have done to him/her if he/she were unconditionally important to you—even when he/she isn't. Love is a relationship in which you give to the other person what he/she needs, not what he/she deserves (said by Frances Busse, a close relative of the author).

When someone is unconditionally important to you in the sense that he/she cannot be substituted by someone else without it making a substantial difference, the relationship (which is not in itself a feeling) gives rise to any of the primary feelings—joy, sorrow, anger, and fear—depending upon what happens within the relation. We are glad when it is good, sad or angry when it is bad, and afraid when the entire relationship is threatened. It is precisely because the other person is important that we feel something, and this goes for the so-called negative feelings as well as the joy that is conventionally seen as the love "feeling." Even anger, which many fear in a personal relationship, may be an expression of love and certainly not its opposite. The true opposition to loving would be indifference (see Chapter 16).

Truth is energizing and contactful
The purpose of these reflections is to support the helper in being honest about all his/her feelings (experiences) in the contact, including (in reasonable proportions) some of the traditionally "forbidden" reactions. These so-called forbidden feelings include anger, grief, and fear, but in the minds of many people it is also forbidden to feel and talk about *happiness* in certain contexts. Many helpers will, for example, in the presence of others who may be ill, old, or dying try to stop themselves feeling happy about being healthy or young or surviving. This inner censorship is based on the idea that happiness in such a situation is malicious, which it does not need to be. Or, it may be due to the fear of *nemesis*, i.e. the punishment of destiny if you "gloat" about your good fortune, superior morality, or superior skills. However, it is not possible to *not* feel (experience) whatever you do feel. It is only possible to repress the experience, and repression has damaging effects such as the following.

- It takes energy to the extent that it may lead to exhaustion or depression.

- The energy that is repressed may turn into anxiety (see Chapter 3) or guilt. It may, for example, produce an exaggerated sense of guilt in the survivors of an earthquake if they try not to appreciate the fact that they are alive when others died.

- The lack of "positive" emotion reduces emotion altogether and therefore diminishes contact.

Love is a process

All genuine (as opposed to simulated) feelings are conducive to *contact* when they are expressed in connection with whatever else happens in the situation (what you see, hear, and want). Contact is conducive to *love*, because love is an especially intense kind of contact, and because love without contact is only the love of a dream. There is a common denominator for love at all levels of contact, from the most exciting, romantic, and private to the most everyday and professional (if and when that is experienced as love, which is often the case). This common denominator is an intensified experience of being—that *I am*—both in the giver and in the receiver of what happens in the relation. This is also true when what happens is a *confrontation*, as long as what is confronted is what the other person *does*, as opposed to what he/she *is*. (See Chapter 9, where contact is defined as the interface of *different* entities.) The process of love is to:

- see and hear the other person

- tell the other person (in relevant amounts) what you see and hear

- tell the other person (in relevant amounts) how you are impacted by what you see and hear.

So, to love is, from the *process* point of view, essentially to see, hear, and respond. When the so-called negative feelings and other negative reactions (for example, "I cannot," "I will not," see Chapter 7) no longer need to be edited out, it will be possible to love (confirm the existence of) your fellow human being even when you are tired and emotionally at the greatest distance.

> "I see that you are trying to catch my eye, and I hear that you are crying, *and* right now, I do not have an emotion left in me for you or anyone else. I do not have time for you either, because there is something else I *want* to do. You have to manage until I see you again tomorrow."

This passage might be called a nightmare for a caregiver in one of the medical professions in that it expresses exhaustion, lack of resources, and thus minimal care for the patient. It may also be said to be extremely politically incorrect. Nevertheless, the patient will probably experience contact and care, because he/she is seen, heard, and taken seriously by a fellow human being. The caregiver does not make excuses for his/her limitations in the situation but merely states them as facts. In that way, he/she takes his/her own reality as seriously as that of the patient. And he/she keeps the future open for renewed contact by speaking in the "here and now" (present) tense. The road to Hell is paved with excuses. The road to Heaven (contact) is paved with statements (observations).

13 LIFE IS NEITHER FAIR NOR UNFAIR

Life just is until it is no more

People who fight against their growing awareness that guilt/ righteousness and fate are not congruent in life should not be helped to deny what they are discovering. The consolation is that there is no (such) consolation (Chapter 11). Life is unfair; therefore, it is not (only) your fault that you are suffering.

Confusing pain with punishment

People in great pain or with other severe difficulties are often tormented by guilt. The hospital patient might, for instance, develop the idea that his/her illness is a kind of punishment, even though he/she has not done anything that is worse than the average person. Perhaps this idea is underpinned by religious notions in the person concerned. Even people who claim that they have no religious belief will come up with questions or statements like the following:

"What have I done to deserve this?"

"I think that I/you/he/she deserved better!"

Such remarks reveal the individual's conscious or semi-conscious spiritual frame of reference. It is the idea that life is fair in that we get what we deserve. If you are good (proper, thoughtful, and conscientious) you may expect good things to happen to you. If you are bad (sloppy, unreliable, and selfish) you may expect bad things to happen to you. Sometimes it is a question of moral goodness or badness, and other times it may be a question of good eating habits, psychological insight, and other qualities or lifestyles. These are in themselves neither moral nor immoral but they come to function as some kind of merit or lack of it, leading to the reward or punishment of fate. If a person in distress is able to stick to the idea that "you get what you deserve" and seems to be getting some comfort from it, the helper should probably not disturb him/her with arguments to the contrary. It is different if the afflicted him/herself has begun to see through the construction of "the just reward" and appeals to the helper to restore it. The helper might feel obligated to produce an answer to support the view that is about to be given up, which might be hard, especially if he/she does not share that particular world view. I would advise the helper not to try to do this. That might sound something like this:

"I also do not think it is fair."

"I don't know what to tell you because personally, I do not think it works that way."

First, it is never possible to turn doubt into belief merely by contradicting the disbelief of the doubter. Second, it is not possible to argue for long against the obvious, and the afflicted is right in his/her dawning insight that life is not fair. Anyone who opens his/her eyes and ears can see that many bad people have good lives, and many good people come to very bad ends. And if anyone has told us it is not so, they have lied to us. Life *is* unfair, or rather, it is neither fair nor unfair. It just *is* until it is no more. The notion of justice is a social construction that nature knows nothing about. Nature's fairness is of another kind. Its rules apply to anyone regardless of what they own, who they are, what they have done, and what they believe. Very democratic, actually!

The Christian view on the justice and injustice of life
Some people seem to perceive the Christian religion as a system that guarantees that good people will have good lives and the bad will fare badly. As long as they seem to draw comfort from such an idea, it is hardly the right or duty of the helper to question it. But if the afflicted run into problems with it and appeal to the helper for assistance on a Christian theological level, it may be useful to remind them what Jesus Christ himself taught on the matter of guilt and fate. In the Sermon on the Mount (Matthew 5, 45) he says that God "makes his sun rise on the evil and on the good, and sends rain on the just and on the unjust." In other words, the founder of the Christian religion also confirms that the laws of nature are not congruent with the laws of morality. According to him, we cannot manipulate God into helping us by doing good or prevent him from helping us by doing bad. Therefore, we may well ask God for what we *need*, but it is not particularly Christian to try to manipulate God, Love, Life, or Fate by telling God what we *deserve*.

Explanation is no comfort

The lack of justice is both a difficulty and a relief. The difficulty is that we can only control our fate to a certain degree, so we may have to settle for something other than what we would have wanted. But there is a certain amount of relief in accepting what is real, even when it is difficult and painful. It is easier to *know* what somehow you do know than to try to repress the knowledge. Then you know what you have to cope with, and if the helper also accepts the reality of your experience (not necessarily objectively but as an experience), you are less lonely and are reassured that you are not crazy to be feeling what you feel.

It may also be a great relief that not everything that happens to you is your own fault. It would not give much comfort to be convinced that all your suffering was self-inflicted, which would be the consequence if you only got what you deserved. Another consequence would be that you would never get anything for free: no Christmas or birthday gifts and no one falling in love with you because of your dimples or funny nose. When the Greek philosopher Socrates had been sentenced to death for something he was innocent of, his friends lamented over the injustice of that. But Socrates' reply was the question, "Would you rather have wanted me to be guilty?" His reply showed that it is not the *injustice* of the suffering that is the real problem; it is the suffering in itself. There would not be any consolation in an explanation that the experienced injustice in "reality" (whose reality?) is justice. The real consolation would be for the pain to go away or, in the absence of that, the helper's empathy with the reality of the suffering.

Something similar applies to the question of meaning and meaninglessness. It is hoped that everything that destroys life and love is just as meaningless as it is experienced. It is hoped that it will never be possible to explain evil in such a way as to make it reasonable or acceptable. And it is hoped that the afflicted may continue to find, in the midst of meaningless situations, meaningful contacts with sympathetic people, and, if they are religious, with a god who is supportive rather than punitive. (See the example in Chapter 18.)

14 BLAME

The flip side of power

"Guilt" also means "responsibility." "Responsibility" also means "power." So, if you feel guilty in a situation where you didn't have the power to avoid it and you don't have the power to rectify it, it is a false or neurotic kind of guilt. Try instead to find out whom you are angry at (or what you are happy about, angry about, or afraid of).

Too little and too much guilt

Earlier we dealt with how people in distress tend to conclude from feeling bad that they must at some point have done something bad. "What have I done to deserve this?" they say, assuming a cause-and-effect relationship between moral conduct and illness and accidents. That is taking too much guilt/responsibility upon yourself. You are not responsible for the hazards of events or the blindness of the forces of nature.

On the other hand, sometimes the troubled person assumes too little guilt/responsibility. He/she may be dimly aware that he/she was, at least in part, responsible for the negative outcome of some action but refuse to face it even though the repressed awareness continues to draw energy in the form of anxiety, depression, and making up excuses. When does a person accept too little responsibility/guilt in connection with a certain course of events? The criterion is that the person being blamed underestimates the amount of influence he/she has had on what happened.

Guilt is the price of choice—the issue is whether what you get is worth what you pay
When the awareness of guilt does arise—perhaps when somebody points out some particularities of behavior and expressions in the helpee that might signal an inner conflict—there is only one course of action that might prove redemptive. That is for the helpee to face his/her guilt/responsibility and live with it. Guilt and responsibility are two sides of the same coin, and responsibility is a word of honor even when what you did was anything but honorable. Owning up to your responsibility sets you free. Although it doesn't set you free from care about what you did and how it affected other people, it leaves you free to reengage in life and look ahead instead of trying to change the past. Trying to deny your responsibility, in contrast, ties you to your excuses and adds the burden of shame to the burden of guilt.

Guilt, i.e. the blame of others and/or your own regret for damage done, may in part result from accidents and unforeseeable circumstances, which is usually the lesser problem when it comes to an individual's assumption of co-responsibility for what has happened. But we may also incur guilt by *choice*, i.e. as part of the price for doing or taking what we wanted even though we were aware that somebody else thought we should have done or taken something else. Clients in therapy are often concerned with how they can get what they want without making anybody upset and without doing damage to their self-image. These individuals need to face the fact that "there is no free lunch." Change comes at a price—guilt, anxiety, effort, pain—and what you get for what you pay, including being "bad," may sometimes be worth the price. The gain might be your freedom from an oppressive relationship where the other person is threatening to commit suicide if you leave, or it might be the freedom to pursue your natural endowments rather than trying to fulfil your parents' ambitions.

If what you get for what you pay is *not* worth the price—for example losing contact with people you love—you would be wise to make another choice. So, making a good choice calls for some thinking and evaluation—"scanning" as the Gestalt therapists say. Automatically "doing your own thing" is not a better (more liberating) solution than automatically doing whatever would please somebody else. Usually, rigid, one-sided patterns of behavior are not constructive, but flexibility is. The key to a relevant course of action is making aware, responsible, balanced choices in the concrete situation, having come to accept that *to incur guilt is also one of your options.*

Real and unreal assessments of guilt

Guilt may be real or "existential" or it may be unreal or imaginary (even though the experience of having a bad conscience is painfully real). "Existential" in this context means that responsibility is an inextricable part of our existence on this planet. The making of choices is part of life, our choices have consequences, and when the consequences are destructive we experience guilt unless we suffer from some character disorder. "Unreal" is the experience of being guilty when it is not proportionate to any real damage that a person has inflicted or to the power he/she had to prevent it. Exaggerated feelings of guilt come from exaggerated ideas about your influence on (power over) the chain of events leading to the damage in question.

The key to distinguishing between real and unreal guilt is, in other words, to look at the power issue. Without influence (power), there can be no responsibility, and without responsibility, there can be no real guilt. This helps to understand why people are often unwilling to let go of their feelings of guilt and even look for guilt/responsibility, such as by asking, "What have I done to deserve this?"

Not all or nothing
We are usually neither totally powerless nor in full control over the events that we get blamed for or blame ourselves for. Reality lies somewhere between these extremes. If the widow of a husband who committed suicide insists that "It was all my fault. I should not have been so hard on him," it is an assertion of omnipotence on her part and reduces the husband to a puppet without any will of his own. That is unreal and it is the opposite of defending the memory of the deceased. The, probably well-intentioned, widow should be helped to see this. On the other hand, if she claims that "It was certainly not my fault" (or a misguided friend attempts to comfort her with the statement that "It was certainly not your fault"), she denies that she had any importance and value for the deceased. That is also unreal, and once she comes to be aware of the consequence, she would probably rather be co-responsible to a limited extent for her husband's death than see herself as "nobody" in their relationship.

66

The helping dialogue may assist the helpee in making a realistic distinction between the co-responsibility that comes from having (some) influence on the one hand, and the non-responsibility for circumstances beyond his/her control on the other. People are, as mentioned above, not always as interested in giving up their exaggerated guilt feeling as the therapist or pastor might expect them to be. Having a bad conscience for what I did may be an extremely heavy burden, but as long as I think I was the one who did it (not just some of it), a hope (rational or not) might arise that I could also somehow undo it. The confronting *and* redeeming statement from the helper might be:

"You don't have that much power."

"How does it feel to have so much power?"

Guilt and repression
Even if the helpee intellectually accepts the above reasoning about the link between power and guilt/responsibility, he/she may continue to *feel* (experience) more guilt than what is real according to the perception of the facts. Phenomenology takes experience seriously, stating that in *practice* (or existentially speaking) nobody comes closer to reality than in his/her experience of it. This is true even when the experience is a result of an irrational interpretation by the perceiver of what he/she senses or when the perception itself is flawed (pathological) as, for instance, in the case of a paranoid projection. At this point, the phenomenological existential therapist or counsellor may widen his/her perspective from the immediate present and obvious facts to include what is veiled in the history of the helpee. In doing so, the Gestalt therapist would not so

67

much be interested in the psychoanalytical themes of past traumas, developmental stages, and issues of transference but would deal with the client's history of *learning* about the world and their place and function in it. In other words, how did we learn who we are in the world such as it is—according to how we have learned to perceive it?

For instance, the Gestalt therapist might ask, "Where/ How did you learn that everything is your responsibility?"

And "What is good and what is bad for you about this idea?" (Maintaining a glorified ego at the cost of chronic exhaustion.)

And the Gestalt therapist might offer some insight into the processes of guilt and shame, such as:

> "Shame means you are not allowed to be who you are, whereas guilt means you are not allowed to do what you do. As long as you think you can do something to change what you are, you will feel guilt (about not doing enough) on top of the shame. When, instead, you give up improving what you are, you will have only the shame, and that is an improvement. Support to endure that shame comes from identifying with whatever is shameful. When you stop trying to be 'good enough,' you come to be as good as you are."

The exaggerated or "unreal" guilt comes (like other forms of anxiety, see Chapter 3) from not being who or where you are. The dynamics are that shame causes repression of basic feelings, desires, thoughts, memories, and values. These are the phenomena that represent *being* as opposed to *doing*. Often it will be some form of anger that is repressed, but it may also be joy, fear, and sorrow.

What, then, is the redemption from shame? The redemption is to identify with whatever is shameful—the "shadow," as C. G. Jung would put it. Not spitefully, as in "I'll show you!" That would leave you reactive (rather than proactive) to the opinion of the other party in the dialogue and to the phenomenon of shame as such. You would, in other words, still be chained by the shaming rather than free to exist in the world even as a shameful person. A statement of fact would make a difference, for instance:

> "Yes, this is what I do feel, do want, do fear, do hope, do remember. I am not particularly proud of it, and sometimes I wish I were different. And I am not."

At that point, the troubled person will *experience* the liberating effect of facing the reality of what *is* even when that reality is not what you would want. "The truth shall make you free," as the Bible says (John 8, 32). Apparently, that is not just a statement for religious people but also realistic psychology for everybody.

An example could be a widow who is angry at her late husband because he has "left" her by dying. She might try to repress this anger because it is irrational to be angry at someone who had no choice in what happened and because she fears it would show her love for the late husband to be less than perfect. So instead of being overtly angry, she might experience an amount of guilt toward the husband that is excessive in view of how the two of them actually lived together.

For this woman, it might be helpful to be made aware that anger is not the opposite of love but that it may, in fact, be an expression of love (see Chapter 12). The helper might, for instance, say something like:

"It is not strange that you are angry about losing him. You loved him!"

In that way, the helper helps the helpee to know what she already knows but hasn't seen the consequences of.

Being guilty is not a feeling, but a relationship that causes feelings

It should be noted that the so-called guilt "feeling" is not a feeling in the sense of the basic feelings (joy, sorrow, anger, and fear). Guilt is, like love, a *relationship* (see Chapter 12). Guilt is where one person *owes* something to another, either as payment for something good he/she has received (gratitude) or as reparation for a loss or damage he/she has caused to the other person. This "energetic" relationship gives rise to feelings in the distinct sense of *emotions* rather than the broader usages such as sensations, evaluations, intuitions, opinions, and likes/dislikes.

When the relationship is that "I must pay for the dent I made in your car," the feelings involved for me may be *fear* of punishment, *anger* at you for your demand of payment/reparation, *grief* for the damage inflicted, and maybe also *grief* for the loss of self-esteem (I thought I was a better driver or more ready to admit to my mistakes). I might even experience some malicious *joy* over the damage I inflicted on your car as in, "I got you and you had it coming!"

The so-called guilt "feeling" is, in other words, a combination of any or all of the basic feelings of gladness, sadness, madness, and fear. Most prevalent in what is generally understood by "bad conscience" or "feeling guilty" is probably *fear*—the fear of retaliation. The particular mixture of the various emotions depends on the intellectual appreciation of what it means to be guilty in the particular situation. Being in debt/having done damage to a close relative or friend may be very different from having done it to a superficial contact or an enemy.

The guilt experience that is false because it comes from repressions and not from actual damage will often disappear on deeper reflection about the underlying feelings associated with the guilt. A constructive question from the helper might be, for example:

"Whom are you angry at?"

15 FORGIVING DOES NOT UNDO THE DAMAGE DONE

Forgiving re-establishes the relationship despite the damage

Forgiving means that love conquers the past, not that the past has been changed. Nobody can do that. Forgiving is not the same as forgetting.

Forgiving may be very powerful for a troubled person to help him/her towards a reconciliation in relationship to old and new conflicts. However, it is important to be clear about what forgiving actually is and what it is not. It is a misunderstanding to believe that forgiving means the removal of guilt; it does not. It may change the experience of how it is to be guilty in a particular relationship (the "subjective" guilt), but the actual fact of the guilt (and here the "objective" guilt) cannot be changed. If somebody has caused an injury to somebody else, that fact will remain for all of eternity. Time cannot be reversed. The person injured in a traffic accident will never return to an uninjured state, even if he/she may regain some or all of his/her physical capacities from before the accident. And the dead will not return to life, even if there is some kind of reconciliation between the person responsible for the death and the survivors. What forgiveness may achieve is some degree of re-establishment of the relationship between perpetrator and victim that was damaged by the injury.

In a partnership, an instance of unfaithfulness will always continue to be part of the history of that relationship. The partners may, however, change the significance of what happened, so that instead of blaming one another or seeking divorce they choose to stay together and develop the relationship. It might even further that development when both parties take seriously what the incident has revealed about the weaknesses and strengths of their relationship. That would be reconciliation or forgiveness in *practice*, even if the people involved (wisely) avoid using such solemn words to describe what is going on. They might talk about "forgetting" what has happened, but the point about forgiving is not having a bad memory. The point is not to use the guilt as a means of gaining power over the other but instead acting *as if* the damage had not happened. Forgiving means giving up your revenge. We may forget, but we cannot *choose* to forget. However, we do have a choice as to how to deal with what we have not forgotten.

Forgiving is not the same as not being angry
We cannot choose not to be angry, but we have a choice as to how to deal with our anger. We are angry until we get what we want, and we cannot choose not to want what we do want. But we may choose to make do without some of what we want in the interest of something we want even more, i.e. the preservation of a valuable relationship. And we

may choose to give up our revenge or demand for reparation even if, at some level, we would want it and deem it to be what we have coming to us. We may choose to give up our revenge *despite* the fact that we are still angry, sorry, or afraid because of what has happened. Forgiving does not mean that one should be (or pretend to be) indifferent about the damage done. When that becomes clear it usually gets easier to forgive and to progress in the relationship.

For nurses, among others, this means that they do not have to deny their anger at being abused by a patient, patient's relative, colleague, or superior. They may express their anger directly, for instance by saying:

> "Yes, now that you ask, I am still upset about what you did/said the other day, and I will try to put it behind me so it will not get in the way of the job that we have to do together."

> "I am still too upset to talk about what happened, and when I have calmed down I will want us to talk it through."

In both cases, the offended person admits to ("owns") his/her anger *and* communicates that there is an opening for a working relationship—or even a friendly one—at some point, despite the anger. For the offender, this will be a clear statement of the boundaries of the offended *and* a confirmation of the importance of the relationship for him/her. You do not need to formulate your anger (your preference for a different behavior) in terms that pose a threat to the relationship ("If you don't give me what I want I am leaving you!") and you do not need to interpret a statement of the other person's preference ("I want you to...!") as that kind of threat.

Forgiving is a process

Both the above examples are illustrations of the non-sentimental, real, true, and mature understanding of what the solemn and often misunderstood word "forgiving" means in practice. It means not cutting the other person off even when you need time for the *process* that reconciliation is. When you realize that, like most other processes, this does not benefit from being forced, it generally becomes easier to carry through. Or, as a minimum, "forgiving" means live and let live, i.e. giving up your revenge even if you do set a limit for the other and say, "I'll never see you again!"

All that applies to the caregiver or helper also applies to the helpee. People who are troubled because they want to forgive a relative but think they can't will often realize that, in practice, they have done it *already* by maintaining the relationship with the person in question. The revelation is that there can be anger and forgiveness *at the same time*, and when people realize that they do not have to make their anger go away, they stop blaming themselves for being "unforgiving." This, in turn, will tend to make them less angry precisely at the moment when they acknowledge their anger, all in accordance with the law of paradoxical change.

16 AND OR BUT

The small words with the large effect

The word "but" functions in practice as a (partial) denial of a previous sentence. "But" also implies a breach of logic or at least convention in the sequence of the two clauses. However, the "logic" is often non-existent in reality and the convention frequently needs to be challenged. The sentence "I love you, but I am angry with you" is conventional, but the logic is as bad as in the sentence "It is March, but it is Wednesday."

"But" as denial

You will notice that the word *and* is frequently italicized in the examples in the following section. It is done in places where most people would spontaneously be inclined to say *but* instead of *and*. The point is to draw attention to the great difference the interchanging of the two words often makes. It is suggested that at delicate points of a dialogue where precision comes to be vital, the use of "and" is given preference even in some cases where, at first, it may sound somewhat unconventional.

"I love you, *but* I am angry with you."

This sentence shows how *but* in practice works as a denial. The negative content of the second part of the sentence cancels out most of the positive content of the first part. Something different happens when the word *and* is used:

"I love you, *and* I am angry with you."

Here both statements retain their full value, and they even emphasize each other. The message will be understood as:

"You clearly love me a lot, since your love is not overshadowed by your anger."

"You must be very angry, since your anger is not overshadowed by a love that great."

In other words, *but* functions negatively for the listener, as a kind of denial. The word is a qualifier or an apology, and you ought therefore to consider whether you *wish* to qualify your statement or apologize for anything.

When this is tried out in a role-playing situation, it always becomes apparent that where *but* should soften up a message and make it easier to listen to, it actually has the opposite effect. The positive part of a message that should help make the negative more palatable ends up being drowned out by the negative. And the attempt to cushion the confrontational part of the message, or avoid taking full responsibility for it, is perceived by the other person as manipulation and therefore as annoying and humiliating.

"But" as a logical conjunction

But presupposes that there is a logical, or "normal," relationship between the two sentences that the word connects—a logic or convention that in this particular instance is, surprisingly, being broken. In other words, there might be a considerable amount of psychology, philosophy, and morality hidden in the use of the word. *But* might communicate the assumption that, "normally," you don't get angry with the person you love. That is, however, bad psychology because it doesn't fit with reality. The reality is that "Precisely because you are so important to me it is extremely difficult for me that you, of all people, do/don't do... Otherwise I might not even notice it" (see Chapter 12). The sentence, "I love you *but* I am angry" is, fortunately, just as meaningless as "It is March, *but* it is Wednesday." Apart from being a reservation or a false excuse, *but* here will promote an unreal perception of how it really is with love and anger. The reality is that they are not opposites but (here in the correct usage as expressing a real contrast) together they are the opposites of indifference.

"But" as hidden moralism

Sometimes *"but"* conveys a hidden moralistic statement of a quite negative nature without the speaker/writer taking full responsibility for it or even being aware of it. Consider the sentence:

"He was poor *but* honest."

This sentence, or something similar, appears in many folk tales, stating in fact that the poor are usually dishonest. The reader may try to interchange *but* with *and* in the examples in Chapter 20. In some instances, *and* will make the sentence quite awkward so don't be rigid about it. On the other hand, awareness about the functions of these words and the development of improved habits in using them will prove that using *and* is surprisingly often the most logical and natural way of joining two sentences.

"And" as key to awareness of ambivalences and the courage to live with them

The underlying psychological/spiritual aspect in the above is that it is important to learn to *live with ambivalences*, that is to say, contradictory feelings and values, and disharmonious experiences. Life in all of its expressions moves in energized fields between the poles of all kinds of opposites, and complete lack of tension is found only in death.

It seems that to a small child, the world is either black or white. Mother is either "sweet" or "stupid." The child may shift rapidly between these opinions, but he/she only seems to be aware of one of them at a time and whichever it is, the child is likely to insist that it was "always" like that and will "forever" stay like that. The mature person, on the other hand, will maintain a background awareness that the person who at the moment is annoying is the same person who at other times is attractive, and he/she will learn from experience that it is even possible to be both *at the same time*. This mature insight is better represented by the conjunction "and" than "but."

Life is wonderful *and* cruel

This may be a caring and realistic sentence to share with a patient or his/her relatives when death is close at hand. There are plenty of other examples of this sort of ambivalent experience. The word "and" undoes the unreal connection established by the "but" between love and being "good enough." Thus, it dismantles a crippling mythology relating to the connection between morality and the laws of nature.

17 HELPING THROUGH DIALOGUE

*If you stay with reality, it is possible
and not too difficult*

*Working with reality is half the work; working against reality
is twice the work.*

When you, as a helper, attempt to be better than you are in *reality*, you will turn out worse than you would if you were to accept your limitations and even put them to good use in the dialogue. When, for example, you think that you:

- are not clever enough, it is because you are not dumb (constructively ignorant, without prejudice, open) enough

- are not good enough, it is because you are not bad (honest) enough

- are not working hard enough, it is because you are not lazy enough (you are too obliging and meddlesome) and have already done too much

- are not able to give enough, it is because you do not take enough (set no limits and disguise your own wishes or needs in the situation).

Conclusion: a bit of bad makes good better

When, as a helper, you have said and done everything you can in accordance with your "sunny side" (the way you prefer to present yourself to the world) and it only makes matters worse, you and the other person must seek redemption from your "shadow" in the Jungian sense. The good helper is constructively ignorant, laid back, and selfish in the positive sense of being transparent with his/her own wants and limitations in the contact. He/she only knows about the other person what that person tells or shows, he/she helps as little as possible *and* as much as necessary to help the other person help him/herself, and he/she is aware of who he/she is in *reality,* as opposed to the ideal world. That is, aware of his/her sensations, emotions, desires, and limitations in the particular situation. That does not mean that everything that is true in the contact needs to be said. Some mature clinical judgment is called for. But everything you do say should be true. You cannot demonstrate and inspire authenticity without being authentic.

The "working reality"

The conclusion of this chapter is that a good helping dialogue is solidly grounded in the perception of reality, i.e. whatever makes a difference in practice, no matter how difficult that reality might be. You find out which reality is at work in the particular contact by seeing, hearing, feeling, and asking what motivates and inhibits the helpee as well as yourself in connection with the subject matter. In many situations, for example in the hospital's scientific atmosphere, it is important to remember that also *irrational* factors can be very real in the sense of making a difference. The beliefs we have about the world and ourselves in it are not rational. If they were, they would be knowledge, not beliefs. We have many assumptions, tastes, and above all *values* concerning what's good or bad that are not logical and also not illogical. They just *are* and we often hold on to them tightly and argue about them even though it makes no sense to argue about whether red is prettier than blue or why good is better than evil. In this realm, we are beyond the rational but certainly not beyond what works in terms of our motivation and resistance.

Tastes, preferences, beliefs, and values are often presented as "soft," even though in the working reality they may be as "hard" as diamond. That they are "soft" means that they cannot be weighed or measured in the way we do with material objects. But it is these immaterial values that ultimately determine what we do with the material. Values build hospitals, prisons, bridges, and roads, and they make war and peace. They are therefore just as "real" or even more so than the objects they are attached to.

Thinking interferes with sensation

Recognition of what works in reality is impeded by habitual thinking about how things usually are, analytical thinking about why things are that way, and moralistic thinking about how things ought to be. Thinking impedes perception because it is hard to do more than one thing at a time, and you might end up more or less blind and deaf to what is *going on* in the situation if you primarily try to analyze it. So, surprisingly perhaps to some, it is relevant to warn the helper against thinking too much. It is more productive to watch, listen, and react to what is *happening* in the contact than to speculate about it. Speculation is fine if it follows perception, not the other way around.

You are *too* clever when what you think you know gets in the way of what you might get to know about the other person if you allowed yourself to be constructively ignorant and bracket your preconceived ideas. The point is to make him/her aware of the obvious and usually quite simple *close* determinants of behavior, such as "I drink because I like it" (Helper: "What, for instance, do you like about it?"), rather than the sophisticated, complicated, *distant* determinants, such as "I drink because my father hit me" (Helper: "Is your father still alive?"). Some additional examples of questioning the obvious might be:

"Exactly *what* is the problem with not being 'good enough'?"

"What exactly is it that *you* are afraid of, now that you know you are dying?"

(See Chapters 18–21 for more examples.)

Goal-obsessed or process-oriented
The problem for helpers who do not think that they are clever enough is usually that they are *too* clever. "Clever" may mean having wisdom, tolerance, and respect for the other person, and you cannot have too much of that. But a know-it-all stance might easily get in the way of the kind of openness and contact that is the aim of an existential

dialogue and that carries the helping process so much further with so much less effort than a detective-like attempt to find out what the helpee "really" has experienced in some past or "really" is trying to say at the present moment.

It should be noted that the aim here is to identify the ongoing process of what is going on in the dialogue, not to show how the helper might get to some *final outcome* of it. The existential dialogue may be inspired by a certain vision, which may change several times during the encounter, but it is not fixated on moving the counselee to a point that in the mind of one or both of the people is considered "better" or "right." As long as we live, there is no final point of development but always room for more growth (as we existentialists say), and the more we learn, the more we may learn in addition to what we have already learned. The helper who absolutely wants to achieve a "satisfactory" outcome or *closure* wants to achieve too much. If the helpee asks:

"Where do I go from here?"

A good response from the helper would be:

"Let us first talk about where you *are*, and then about where you *want* to go!"

Too much of a good thing is no good!
You may be too clever exactly when you think you are not clever enough, and in a similar way you may be working too hard precisely when you think you are not working hard enough. You are too busy on the other's behalf when you give in to the manipulation of a helpee who is trying to avoid an effort or responsibility that actually belongs to him/herself. When the helper is doing for the other what

he/she is able to do for him/herself, the helper is working *too* hard in the sense that he/she is depriving the help seeker of the opportunity to develop his/her own coping strategies and stamina. One likely outcome is that the client will increase his/her appetite for outside support and hence increase his/her demands on the helper to the point where he/she definitely will fall short of being able to fulfil them.

Similarly, it is possible to be too unselfish precisely when you think you are not as kind and giving as you or the other person would wish. You are too altruistic when you ignore your own sensations of exhaustion or lack of interest (typically because the other person is talking *about* and not *to*) or your emotions, such as your anger at being offended. If you neglect your own needs with regard to being able to function optimally in the situation, you are out of touch with reality—specifically the reality that even helpers are humans—and this will be a substantial loss in the context because it is the humanity that is the key resource in the existential dialogue.

Helping nature to heal itself
When it comes to the existential phenomenological helping dialogue, a good helper is naïve, lazy, and selfish, to put it in somewhat provocative terms. This ideal is possible to achieve for most people but, paradoxically, it may take quite a bit of practice for it to become routine. Much of our habitual thinking about helping points in the opposite direction. On the other hand, the helper will probably quickly begin to notice that with *reality* supporting the process, he/she will get better results (contact) for less work. At the same time, the patient, client, colleagues in the institution, and relatives of the troubled person will experience the contact

as very useful (constructive), i.e. more respectful without being invasive.

If you work *against* reality, you will end up working more than necessary and get less for your effort. But if you work *with* reality, you will achieve more and pay less. The best medical treatment has always been one that supports the natural processes. And what applies to the treatment of the body also applies to the care for the mind and soul, including care in the form of the helping dialogue.

III

Examples

p.89

18 THE MEANING

A dialogue about meaning turns
into something meaningful

The example below is taped from a training session with a group of nurses in advanced communication training. During the dialogue, the trainer addresses both the patient and the helper. A nurse functions in both roles, shifting back and forth between two chairs that represent herself and the patient, respectively. The aim of the training is to increase the trainee's awareness of the *process* of the dialogue in addition to the content. Towards the end, the trainer (the writer) makes some supplementary comments on the theological parts of the dialogue.

Like anything else in this book, this dialogue is meant to be a demonstration of a possible approach to a certain theme or problem, not the one and only way to deal with it. The dialogue might have turned out in numerous other ways that would have been just as "right." There is no guarantee that all patients would react in precisely the same way as the man in the example. The point of the exercise is that the nurse comes to be aware of where and how she blocks contact with patients having religious and existential problems. With increased awareness of her own functioning (process) during a helping dialogue with this kind of content, she will be better equipped to see, hear, and respond to what actually does happen with the patient. As a result of the training, she realizes that she does not have to find a "meaning" for her partner in the dialogue. She, an active Christian believer, also realizes that she does not have to defend God, which would formerly have been her tendency. Both discoveries will tend to make her less apprehensive in the future about religious/existential themes entering the dialogue.

The dialogue is reproduced with the permission of the nurse. It is based on a real situation with one of her patients, but the patient's details have been changed so he cannot be recognized.

Background

The nurse talks with a middle-aged man, Johnson, who suffers from sclerosis. He is paralyzed from his waist down and is in a wheelchair in the nursing home. He is there by his own choice in order not to burden his family. The nurse thinks it might improve his bad mood if he would take part in the various activities of the home, and it frustrates her that he refuses to do so. Some of the remarks in the exercise function as a kind of draft to the finished exchange between nurse and patient. The final text is in bold. P = Patient; N = Nurse; T = Trainer.

P: **This is not a life for a man like me. What's the meaning? Why must I go through this?**

T (to N): How do you react to that? Are you glad, sad, mad, or afraid?

N: Offhand I guess I get a little scared that I won't be able to handle the situation.

T: What will happen if you tell P that? What does not "handing" the situation mean?

N: That I will not be able to say the right words.

T: Aha! This takes the mystery out of the word "handle." It is one of the all-pervasive mysteries of the language of the helping dialogue. "Breakdown" is another one. It suggests a psychotic breakdown, but in practice it usually just means to cry a lot. "Handle" suggests answering in a way that makes everything bad disappear, which is rarely possible. However, in practice, much less will do. It suffices just to react to what the helpee expresses in a way that lets him/her know you have seen and heard him/her. See what happens if you tell P, "I am afraid I don't have an answer for you." That is actually a "contactful" answer, even if we don't know whether it "handles" anything or not.

N: **I am afraid I don't have an answer for you.**

T: What was it like for you to say that? Do you get more, or less, afraid?

N: Less afraid.

T: Yes. Things do not change until we accept them such as they are. Johnson, what is it like for you that your nurse does not have an answer for you?

P: **It's like… I tried to pass it off to you** (N). **What shall I do? What shall I do with my life? I might as well be lying in my grave.**

T (to N): How do you react to that? Do you agree or disagree that he might as well be lying in his grave? What is *your* opinion?

N: I do not think that it is true. I think he could do so much. He is good with his hands, and he could get something out of his life if he would. I have a hunch it is because he doesn't want to.

T: So, what will you say or do now?

N (after a long pause): **If that is so, why aren't you?**

T (impressed): Yes. That is certainly a possibility. A courageous choice *and* in this situation perhaps *too* confrontational. You phrased it as a question—a "why" question. That is usually not as good as a "how" question. And better than all questions are, whenever possible, a *statement*. The statement that would correspond to what you just said would be "In that case, I wonder why you don't take you own life," or better, "I notice that you have not done it yet!"

That would really be a phenomenological response, that is, one that is based on perception without interpretation. But let us go on from what you did say and hear how Johnson responds.

P: **I don't dare to kill myself. I simply don't have the courage.**

T (to P): What is it like for you that the nurse talks to you like that?

P: I am fine with it. She takes me seriously.

T: Yes. This shocking, awful, "un-Christian" reply that made the rest of the class jump is *positive* in Johnson's perception. He likes it. Not necessarily the *content*. "You can't polish shit," as my trainer Tony Horn said, meaning that psychotherapy cannot change what *is* but at best it can change the way in which you deal with it. However, Johnson likes the *process*, that is the authenticity of the helper and hence the contact with her. Now you (N) know that, because you have been sitting in P's chair. You learn a surprising amount about another person by literally putting yourself in his/her place. What will you say or do now?

N (to T): What can one say to that?

T (to N): Where are you? Are you glad, sad, mad, or afraid?

N: I am glad that he thinks we are talking—connecting. I think I will wait for what he says next.

T (to P): The nurse says nothing. She is still there and looks at you. It looks to me as if her eyes are a bit moist. What will you do or say now?

P: **I will not take any more of your time. It's time for you to get your supper.**

T (to P): How is it for you to finish in this way?

P (to T): Not good. I want to talk about this. I need to talk about it.

T (to P): What exactly is it that you would like to talk about?

P (to T): I want the nurse to tell me why...what is the meaning of my life?

T (to N): What are you going to do about the fact that Johnson doesn't want to take any more of your time?

N: **I have enough time.**

T (impressed, moved): Yes. The simplest possible answer— and the best! Or, if you did not have time, "You're right. I do not have time *right now*, and if you want I can come back when I do have time."

T (to P): How are you with the nurse saying that she does have time?

P: That's fine.

T (to P): How will you use that time?

P: **I know quite well…(pause). I was brought up with the idea that God is good. That's what I learned. But…why? Why should this hit me? God can't be good when he allows something like this to happen. I don't feel good!**

T (to N): So, Johnson will use the time to ask you this theological question. You are welcome to counsel with me about what one might answer. Or, you may answer him directly. What do you want to say or do?

N: **I can very well understand that you feel it is hard.**

T (to P): The nurse does not answer your question but says she very well understands that it is hard for you. How are you with that?

P: **What am I supposed to do with that?**

T (to N): Yes. And what do you think the emotions are in that? Is he glad, sad, mad, or afraid?

N: I don't really know.

T: To me, he sounded angry, and if this had been your perception as well, one possibility would have been to share this perception with him—as a statement like "You sound angry." Another one is that you share with him what you *intended* with what you said about understanding him. Did you have in mind that he should be able to *do* anything with it or because of it?

N: No. Not that he should be able to make any use of it. It was more like…an indication of…

T: See what happens if you tell him that!

N: **I didn't expect you to *do* anything. It was just an indication on my part of…kindness** (smiles, slightly embarrassed).

T (speaking for N): …and now that you stop me, I realize that perhaps I do not understand you anyway. But it

95

was an attempt to...meet you. See what happens if you tell him all of that!

N: Johnson, when I say what I just said about understanding you and you say that you can't make any use of that, I realize that maybe I don't understand you anyway. But it was...like...a way of meeting you.

N (to T): I want so badly to tell him, "Johnson, life is not about what happens to you but about how you *take* it. Look at Mrs. Jones in her wheelchair over there. She can't *do* anything but see how she is making everybody at her table happy. They are all talking with one another." That's the kind of thing I have in the back of my mind, and I know it's totally forbidden (laughs).

T (to N): If you begin by clearly stating what you want to talk about and what makes you hesitate (fear of being intrusive, pushy, or irrelevant), this is fine because it is contactful. It is called "turning the stumbling block into a stepping stone." Then at least you meet yourself at the point where *you* are, even if it is not where P is. Now he knows where he may find you if he wants to.

Whenever you find it impossible to put your own stuff in the background, your best option is to put it all the way out by telling the other person something (as little as possible and as much as necessary for the contact to be re-established) about it. That will wash away the grey film of your secrets from your windshield, so to speak, and the helpee will again be clearly visible as your foreground.

It is true also for you, the helper, that you won't change until you accept who, what, and where you are. Now you know what you want, and so does P. And how come you want it?

N: So that Johnson will feel good.

T: Why should he feel good?

N: So I will succeed in my nursing.

T: Now we know what we are talking about!

N (laughs): Yes, otherwise I will feel inadequate.

T: See how it will be for you to tell Johnson, "I just caught myself wanting to console away your misery, so I wouldn't have to bear it for you."

N: **Johnson, I just caught myself in wanting to console away your misery so that I wouldn't have to bear it for you.**

T: These were my words—as a suggestion. Do you experience them as being true for you?

N: Yes.

T: What is it like to tell Johnson the truth?

N: Good!

T: It is no disaster if from time to time you fall back on the conventional strategies of trying to make your patients happy: distraction, word magic, and fake identification (confluence). Nobody has to be perfect, not even professional helpers. However, if this strategic way has been a certain helper's primary approach, it would be advantageous for him/her to supplement it with some dialogue. The dialogue is not in a hurry to get somewhere. It explores what *is* in the here and now, trusting this to be the best possible starting point for whatever may come.

I noticed with appreciation that you let yourself be stopped by the helpee. It was Johnson who stopped you in this case. And I appreciate that you yielded to the truth when you responded with "You are right. I did that."—Let us hear what Johnson will say or do now.

P: **You can't.**

N: **It's good that you say so yourself.**

N (to T): That's what I wanted to tell him…in my moralizing way.

T (to N): Yes.

T (to P): What will you say or do now? Your nurse says, in effect, "Thanks for relieving me from the responsibility for your illness."

P: **I just don't know what to do to get out of this.**

N: **I can't tell you.**

T: Yes. Precisely. You are doing fine! When you don't know what to say or do, then that's what you should say or do. You can't make his sclerosis go away. You also can't make his life go away, and neither can he unless he does something drastic about it. There is no way out for him. Both of you know that, and if you can't talk about that you can't talk about anything in a real (contactful) way.

N: **Johnson, I don't see a way out for you. You can't make the sclerosis go away, and as long as you do not do anything actively to die you will go on living. So, there is nothing for you to do. That also means that there is nothing you must do.**

T: Clearly! When there is nothing you *can* do, there is also nothing you *must* do. It is very simple, really, in terms of language, grammar, and formal logic, but people often overlook it. They are so preoccupied with their frustration over being powerless that they don't notice the relief inherent in the fact that there is nothing they must do in the situation. The good part of being powerless is that you are not at fault!

How is it for you to say what you just said? (Pause.) I know very well that you would want him to do some occupational therapy and that kind of thing, but that's not really where we are at right now.

N: Oh no. We are talking about how we might make the sclerosis go away and life turn wonderful or disappear some night when he is asleep. As far as that goes, there is nothing he or I can do, and it is good to confirm that. It is true.

T (to P): How are you with that?

P: **It's good to get that settled.**

T (to N): He seems relieved. What's happening to you?

N: **I sense your relief, and it makes me glad.**

T (to P): How concerned are you at this point about "the meaning of life" and "Why me?" and "I might as well be dead"?

P: I'm not very concerned about that right now.

T (to N): Try to ask him about what is meaning*ful* (as opposed to the meaning) for him right now. That's a somewhat different way of talking about it.

N: **What is meaningful for you right now, Johnson?**

P: **That I can talk with you like this. The contact.**

T (to N): How do you think it happened that you got that kind of contact?

N: **What is it that makes it meaningful for you?**

P: **It's because you finally met me.**

N: **So, what's the meaning of life?**

P: **Contact!**

T: Yes. Closeness, contact, warmth. In one word: love. Nobody asks for the meaning of life when he/she gives or receives love, so love must be the meaning we look for when we ask for "the meaning." It's not about meaning in the sense of "plan" or "purpose." That kind of meaning gives little or no comfort or support when the chips are down. It's about meaning in the sense of what's meaningful, i.e. what has *value* and gives *fullness* so that life is worth living even when it hurts. If you are lucky, you may experience some of that even if you suffer from sclerosis. (Pause.) Try and ask him what's left for him if he doesn't even have that?

N: **What's left for you, Johnson, if you don't even have that?**

P (after a long pause and as he straightens up and looks the nurse firmly into the eye): **Then I will survive anyway!**

N (moved): **Yes. You don't even have closeness, contact, and warmth, and you survive. What is it that's left?**

P: **Just the fact that I am, nothing else.**

T (slightly trembling, deeply impressed): Precisely! *I am!* That remains. I am what I am. I am Johnson. I have sclerosis. I am until I am no more. It is vital to find out that love is the most important thing in life — except for the one thing that is even more important, which is the very fact that we *exist*. Being here is the precondition for our meeting and experiencing full contact. When Moses at the burning bush in the desert asked for God's name, the answer was a word that means "I am." This is as far as anyone of us gets, *and* it is far enough.

Without the in-between prompts and explanations, the resulting dialogue reads as follows:

P: This is not a life for a man like me. What's the meaning? Why must I go through this?

N: I am afraid I don't have an answer for you.

P: It's like... I tried to pass it off to you (N). What shall I do? What shall I do with my life? I might as well be lying in my grave.

N (after a long pause): If that is so, why aren't you?

P: I don't dare to kill myself. I simply don't have the courage.

P: I will not take any more of your time. It's time for you to get your supper.

N: I have enough time.

P: I know quite well... (pause). I was brought up with the idea that God is good. That's what I learned. But...why? Why should this hit me? God can't be good when he allows something like this to happen. I don't feel good!

N: I can very well understand that you feel it is hard.

P: What am I supposed to do with that?

N: I didn't expect you to *do* anything. It was just an indication on my part of...kindness (smiles, slightly embarrassed).

N: Johnson, I just caught myself in wanting to console away your misery so that I wouldn't have to bear it for you.

P: You can't.

N: It's good that you say so yourself.

P: I just don't know what to do to get out of this.

N: I can't tell you. Johnson, I don't see a way out for you. You can't make the sclerosis go away, and as long as you do not do anything actively to die you will go on living. So, there is nothing for you to do. That also means that there is nothing you must do.

P: It's good to get that settled.

N: I sense your relief, and it makes me glad. What is meaningful for you right now, Johnson?

P: That I can talk with you like this. The contact.

N: What is it that makes it meaningful for you?

P: It's because you finally met me.

N: So, what's the meaning of life?

P: Contact!

N: What's left for you, Johnson, if you don't even have that?

P (after a long pause and as he straightens up and looks the nurse firmly into the eye): Then I will survive anyway!

N (moved): Yes. You don't even have closeness, contact, and warmth, and you survive. What is it that's left?

P: Just the fact that I am, nothing else.

19 EXPANDING ON THE CONCEPT OF MEANING

"Meaning" means "value." What makes your life worth living?

Insight into what causes a disaster is not much comfort to the afflicted. Contact with another person and awareness of the values of whatever remains after the disaster are.

"Meaning" is one of the mystifying concepts that comes up in talking with people in crisis. What does it mean? It always implies "context." Nothing has meaning, i.e. increases understanding or communicates a message, by itself alone. A single note cannot tell you whether a piece of music is high or low pitched or in the major or minor key—you need to hear a few bars of the music to do that. A single letter is just a pencil mark on a piece of paper and communicates nothing. Only in connection with other letters does it begin to gain meaning as part of a word, and when placed in a sentence that word will get its precise connotation in the particular context.

When people are struck with disaster, they typically experience that their customary context has collapsed. "It seems so meaningless" means "My life is not coherent any longer" and therefore also "not comprehensible." This tends to cause deep anxiety, like when a pilot runs into a heavy fog and finds it hard to do what is needed to prevent a crash. So, people in crisis grope for a meaning, i.e. a coherency, something that fits together, or in Greek a *system*, meaning literally something that stands together.

The question is which system? Typically, people first look for the connection between cause and effect. "What have I done for this to happen to me?" they ask. It may sound religious—related to sin and punishment—but it may also be an expression of magic thinking, which is a primitive form of science. The interest behind the question is to find a necessary connection between what's happening now and what happened earlier, which, if found, would make it possible to control destiny. "If I am ill because I have done bad, I can be well by doing good" seems to be the argument and, in consequence, people begin their surprising search for something to feel guilty about—as if they did not have sufficient pain already.

Many helpers have felt obliged to go along with this mindset and worked hard trying to find causalities that would answer the helpee's "why" questions. I advise giving this up. If the helpee did end up with an explanation (other than the medical) as to why he/she is ill or about to die, it would probably not make him/her feel any better. It is too late to be good retroactively, and no one can gain magic control over his/her present or future by eating right, behaving right, or thinking right. Perhaps most importantly, whether there is an explanation or not, if the afflicted has lost the "meaning" (the meaningful, the valuable, what motivated him/her) of his/her life, then of course he/she is *right* in that his/her life at the moment is just as meaningless as it feels. Therefore, it would be truly meaningless if the helper denied it.

This leads us to a totally different kind of connectedness that does support us in staying alive even when life is horrible. It is, as the dialogue in Chapter 18 demonstrated, the *contact* with people, objects, and actions that have *value* for the person in need. In the example, the nurse helps the patient to shift from the cause-and-effect connection to the me-and-my-values connection when she asks, "What is meaning*ful* (again, experienced as opposed to a more speculative or metaphysical kind of meaning) for you (the patient) at this moment?" She might also have used the word "valuable," i.e. worth living for. The patient's answer is that the *contact*, i.e. his connection with you at this moment, gives coherence to his life so that it makes sense (is worth it) to stay alive even now.

What might support a person *now* is not looking for causes in the past ("What have I done?") or purposes in the future ("What am I supposed to learn from this?"). What gives the courage to live and the strength to die *now* are the values (the love) that are worth living and, if necessary, dying for. Finally, in the example in Chapter 18 it turned out that connecting and identifying with one's desire to stay alive just for the sake of staying alive in itself supports a person in doing just that. *Being* itself takes precedence over not being when you give up trying to change what is and what you are. There is no rush towards death when you take seriously the fact that what you have is all that you get.

The choice is between the life that you have or no life. No one else can make that choice for you.

If realizing this is not sufficient to rekindle the helpee's desire to be alive, the helper might try to engage him/her in some fantasizing about what might make his/her life worth living. The subjunctive is less frightening than the indicative. Then the two of them might look at (scan) how much of the fantasy could come to be reality, and what it would take to accomplish that. "*This* is your life. What might and what will you *do* with it?" With these questions, the constructively lazy and ignorant helper avoids being confluent with the afflicted, i.e. he/she stays aware of who has power over and hence responsibility for what. You do not need to be particularly smart, energetic, or good in order to do that. All it takes is eyes, ears, and enough honesty to put into words what both parties have already seen and heard. When you help the other person to know what he/she already knows, you return to him/her the support he/she already has but has lost sight of. That will function *organically* in contrast to transfusions and prostheses.

20 POSSIBLE NEW ANSWERS

*When your good old answers do not lead
to the kind of contact you want*

Many "old" answers are contradictions that attempt to balance out the negative questions and statements of a helpee with a positive response. Occasionally, that kind of reaction may help the afflicted to look at his/her situation in a somewhat broader perspective, but often it just leads to a loss of contact. The "new" answers below are all based on acceptance of the experience of the other person. *They are not the only "right" answers*, but it is usually helpful to have a variety of choices, and that is also the case when talking with a person in great difficulties.

Patient, client, counselee, help seeker = P; Helper = H. The phrases a, b, c, etc. are meant as alternatives. In some cases, they may also be combined. Fantasy is the only limit.

P: I am not good enough.
H: a. What is it that you are not good enough at/for?

b. It must be hard for you that you are not as good as you would like to be.

c. What is it that you can't do/can't get because you are not good enough?

d. You can't get love by being good enough.

e. No, *that* (something concrete) you obviously are/were not good enough to accomplish.

f. (If you are a close person) I don't care. You are the one that I want.

P: I'm nothing.
H: True. You are not a thing.

P: I'm useless.
H: So are newborn babies and the lilies of the field. How come you want to be useful rather than just to *be*?

P: It seems so unfair.
H: I hope it is. If not, all of it would be your own fault. Life is not fair. It is also unfair that you are born in the first place and that you are living in a country where we get enough to eat.

P: What's the meaning?
H: I see none. I hope there is no meaning with this. Life is full of things that I for my part can only live with because I hope they are as meaningless as they seem. Wars, for instance.

P: It seems so hopeless.
H: Hope is sometimes more of a curse than a blessing. How would it be for you to let go of it?

P: I don't know if I want to live any longer.
H: I also don't know if I would want it in your place. I do
hope that you will choose to live.

P: It's all a pile of shit!
H: a. It sounds like you are angry/sad. What is most shitty
right now?
b. Yes.

P: Nobody listens to me!
H: I don't like that you call me nobody. *I* am listening to
you right now.

P: I'm so scared of dying!
H: a. Yes.
b. You owe that to life. What are you most scared of
right now?

P: I hate being a burden.
H: a. Yes!
b. You *are* a burden. That's what I am here for.

P: Excuse me for being so much trouble!
H: a. You *are* a lot of trouble *and* as you see, I can stand it.
b. It's actually more trouble if on top of it I also have to
excuse you.

P: I'm so afraid of being a burden to my children.
H: You *are* a burden to them. Once, they were a burden to
you. How was that?

P: You don't understand me.

H: No, probably not entirely. *And* I can both see and hear that you are miserable.

P: I'm so afraid.

H: a. Yes!

    b. I can see it and hear it. What are you most afraid of *right now*?

P: I have so much anxiety.

H: Anxiety comes from not being where you are. Where are you right now?/What is going on with you right now?

P: I can't find my optimism any more.

H: Stop looking for it. Maybe it will come back, but you can't make it.

P: They tell me to pull myself together.

H: a. How are you with that?

    b. If they told me something like that I would get mad. What does it do to you?

P: I can't make it.

H: What is it that you have to make? Time passes, whether you make it or not.

P: I can't make it (surviving).

H: It does look serious. Do you want to talk about what you would like to have taken care of, in case you don't make it?

P: I feel so powerless.

H: You have no power over this. And if you are powerless and try not to be, you'll end up with two problems rather than one. What would it be like for you to let go of the power that you don't have anyway?

P: It's easy for you—you are young and well.

H: Yes, and I do appreciate it. In a place like this (hospital) you don't take your good health for granted.

P: Believe me, it's not fun getting old.

H: a. I also do not look forward to it.

b. I can see it's hard for you. I hope I'll get off easier when it comes to be my turn.

P: I feel it's all my fault.

H: a. You don't have that much power.

b. What is it like to have that much power?

P: Can you help me?

H: a. Maybe. What is it that you would like me to help you with?/What is it you hope to get from me?

b. No. Only by being here.

c. No. As far as I can see, there is nothing I can do about it. *And* I stay.

21 COMMENTARY TO THE "NEW" ANSWERS

The one-liners above have from time to time given rise to objections like "You can't talk to people like that," or "If I were that patient, I would have got really mad." It should be noted that these objections have all been made by people who have only heard or read *about* these suggested responses and not themselves tested them in practice. Let me emphasize again that the statements and counter-questions are not an infallible manual to the perfect dialogue. There is hardly anything that is always right, nor anything that is always wrong—except being fixated on getting it all right every time. The purpose of the examples is to show what might be possible and constructive in a helping dialogue, even if it contrasts or conflicts with customary ideas about what is "permissible," or about the usefulness of trying to comfort away negative experiences. What, in a given, concrete context is "right" to do or say must depend on the context and the "feeling" (sense) of the particular helper as to what the particular contact can bear. There is no guarantee ahead of time that the helper will not make a mistake, but it is never too late to say, "excuse me," and when, as the helper, you demonstrate that you can own up to your imperfections, you give a very positive message to the helpee.

It should also be noted that all the examples in this book are *born out of practice*, so to insist that they wouldn't work would be like insisting that the bumble bee is so heavy and its wings so small that it couldn't possibly fly. These *suggested* responses have been shaped in dialogue with people in severe predicaments and great suffering. Again and again, they have been tested in "chair work" in connection with the writer's training and supervision of largely any category of students and experienced practitioners in the helping professions. And so far, everyone who him/herself has tried out these responses, or some that are similar, in practice has agreed that it is a relief for both parties in the dialogue to give up manipulations, avoidances, cosmetics, magic, and, above all, ambitions.

You might expect the recipient of such straight talk to be offended, but reality proves that it is not the case. It is a relief to both people to stop manipulating because deep down inside we all seem to know that what we gain through manipulation is ill gained. Therefore—often to our surprise—it is better to do without. "The truth will set you free," and miraculously that always works two ways.

The above suggestions are well worth *considering* as useful alternatives to the responses that as a helper you are most familiar with already and that are likely to serve your purposes well in many or most situations. The most important aspect of the examples is the *process* they illustrate. It is: *authentic presence based on clear perceptions and honesty* concerning the helper's own motivation and limitations in the encounter. The written notes are not the tune and the map is not the territory. But if you will endeavor to "tune in" to what's going on at the contact boundary between yourself and your partner in dialogue, you will be able to provide the rhythm and phrasing that give the written word meaning and life, and if you are willing to brave the unknown of the in between, you will be able to supply the territory with names, landmarks, and pathways.

REFERENCES

Beisser, A. (1971) "Paradoxical Theory of Change." In Fagan, J. and Shepherd, I. (eds) *Gestalt Therapy Now.* New York: Harper & Row. Available at www.gestalt.org/arnie.htm, accessed on 20 April 2017.

Jung, C. G. (1948) *Die Beziehungen der Psychotherapie sur Seelsorge.* Zürich: Zascher verlag.

BIBLIOGRAPHY

Beisser, A. (1971) "Paradoxical Theory of Change." In Fagan, J. and Shepherd, I. (eds) *Gestalt Therapy Now.* New York: Harper & Row. Available at www.gestalt.org/arnie.htm, accessed on 20 April 2017.

Buber, M. (1937) *I and Thou.* New York: Charles Scribner's Sons.

Van Deurzen-Smith, E. (2002) *Existential Counselling in Practice.* London: Sage Publications.

Hostrup, H. (2010) *Gestalt Therapy.* Copenhagen: Museum Tusculanum Press.

Sand, I. (2017) *The Emotional Compass.* London: Jessica Kingsley Publishers.

Jung, C. G. (1948) *Die Beziehungen der Psychotherapie sur Seelsorge.* Zürich: Zascher verlag.

Perls, F. (1969) *Gestalt Therapy Verbatim.* Moab: Real People Press.

Perls, F. (1978) *The Gestalt Approach*. Palo Alto, CA: Science and Behavior Books.

Spinelli, E. (1989) *The Interpreted World*. London: Sage Publications.

Yontef, G. (1993) *Awareness, Dialogue* and *Process*. Highland, NY: Gestalt Journal Press.